Walk Cornwall
Porthleven
& Mullion

Looking over Jangye-ryn beach from Castle Mound at Gunwalloe. The cliffs are typical of slate – a far cry from The Rill & Vellan Head.

Porthleven & Mullion

*Predannack, Mullion, Poldhu to
Porthleven & Trewavas Head*

THE SERPENTINE CLIFFS of **Vellan Head** and **The Rill** are the most imposing on the whole Lizard coastline. Polurrian marks the abrupt end of the rare and unusual rocks of the Lizard and the start of a softer coastline of small inlets and pebbly coves backed by crumbly slate cliffs. **Church Cove** at **Gunwalloe** is one of those places where happy family days are made. It's got all the ingredients needed – an ancient church built implausibly close to the beach, sand dunes to run and hide in and a stream to dam. Stir in legends of wrecked Spanish galleons spilling Aztec treasure chests into **Dollar Cove** and you have a thrilling mix. Even today, silver coins occasionally turn up on the beach. Searching the pebbles for Montezuma's treasure will keep the whole family busy for hours.

Further along the coast and past the cliffs at **Halzephron** – *Hell's Cliffs* in Cornish – the 4 kilometres of flint pebbles that make up Loe Bar is an ideal place for a blowy walk followed by a pint at the Halzephron Inn. The sand and shingle has blocked the estuary of the River Cober to create **Loe Pool**. The wooded walks around the pool are a rare treat in wind blasted West Cornwall where trees are sparse. Car parks dot the banks and creeks so you can tailor the length of the walk to suit your mood.

On a coast as fearsome and sparsely populated as this one, the harbour at **Porthleven** is a rare haven. The harbour quays once stacked with pit props for local mines and kegs of china clay are now busy with visitors to the craft shops, restaurants and artists' studios. This book ends on the granite headland of **Trewavas Head**. Here you get a real flavour of the granite coves to come on the Land's End peninsula.

GETTING AROUND

BUS

The Helston - Lizard Town service will get you within walking distance of the main beaches at Poldhu & Polurrian. Jump off at Mullion Golf Course for Church Cove, Gunwalloe. Jump off at Cury Church & walk across the top of Gunwalloe Marsh to Halzephron.
The Helston - Penzance service will get you to Loe Bar (Penrose Hill stop) & to Porthleven.

Porthleven

PLACES TO VISIT

- Helston Folk Museum. Eccentric collection of all sorts from prehistory to 1960s cookers & toasters, check opening times before you visit
- Flambards Fun Fair
- Back bar of the Blue Anchor in Helston or front bar of the Ship Inn at Porthleven

West Coast of the Lizard

Predannack, Gew-graze, Vellan Head & Kynance

Black cliffs of the West Coast

Helston
Mullion Cove
Predannack
Kynance
Lizard Point

BUS
Helston - Lizard Town bus, jump off at Kynance Garage & walk across Lizard Downs to Kynance Cove.

CAR PARKING
National Trust car parks at Predannack Wollas & Kynance Cove.

FOOD & DRINKS
If you're parking at Predannack, there are pasty shops & cafes in Mullion. If you're parking at Kynance, you'll find food shops, cafes & pubs in Lizard Town plus Kynance Cafe right on the beach.

LOOK OUT FOR...
- Cornish choughs on the cliffs
- Orchids in early summer
- Windmill Farm Nature Reserve – you can enter from A3083 (Map7, B1) or from the footpaths on Lizard Downs
- Harebells at Gew-graze valley in summer

A raw and lonely part of the Lizard coast, almost completely set on serpentine bedrock. **The Rill** (Cornish for *cleft*) and **Vellan Head** (Cornish, *melyn* is *yellow* presumably from the prominent yellow and orange lichens here) are the most impressive cliffs on the Lizard. At **Predannack Downs** the heathland merges with the coast showing how the plants of the downs, like the heathers, have their origins in the natural habitat of the cliffs. There's only a single farm on the 5km (3 mile) stretch of coast between **Pentreath Beach** and **Pol Cornick**, a stark reminder of the infertility of serpentine soils.

Predannack Airfield
The airfield was built in 1941 to defend Cornish coastal towns, particularly the important docks at Falmouth. Radar stations already existed at Dry Tree (Goonhilly) and Trelanvean to detect hostile bombers. Coastal Command flew patrols against U-boats operating in the English Channel and the Bay of Biscay from here. Its remote location was ideal for secrecy. Barnes Wallis did work here on the bouncing bomb for the Dambusters raid and later at the height of the Cold War, it was used for jet fighter development. The Royal Navy took over control in 1958 and it's now a busy satellite field for the Royal Navy air station at Culdrose. It's used mainly for training helicopter pilots, practising helicopter based commando assaults and for crash rescue and fire practice. Old

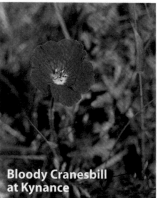

Bloody Cranesbill at Kynance

Gew-graze Cove looking towards the table top flatness of Vellan Head.

jets and helicopters are visible from the footpath that skirts the airfield, they are used for rescue practice. The large mock-up air frame is used for fire practice – when it's in action huge plumes of black smoke can be seen from as far away as Penzance and Falmouth.

Windmill Farm

A large area of Predannack Downs was lost under the runways of the airfield in the 1940s but the peripheral areas of the airfield have been spared and are rich habitats. Cornwall Wildlife Trust have reserves on the north of the airfield at North Predannack Downs, and on the east side of the airfield at Windmill Farm. In one of those beguiling adjacencies that you come across on the Lizard, you can sit watching dragonflies hover in front of you, while Royal Navy helicopters buzz back and forwards overhead. The reserve is farmed to encourage birds and invertebrates and there is a small information centre about Lizard wildlife.

Geology

The serpentine cliffs have a striking tabletop flatness. Stand on top of Kynance Cliff today & you're 70m (230ft) above sea level – but 25 million years ago you would be standing at the bottom of a shallow sea. It's the sea that has planed the serpentine flat & as it's very resistant to erosion, little has changed since apart from it being pushed upwards by earth movements. At Crousa Downs near Coverack, which is 30m (100ft) higher still, there are deposits of rounded sea pebbles stranded on top of the downs.

Flora.

There's an unusual plant survival on the valley sides – *Prostrate Juniper*. It's a plant mainly of dry mountainous places, both sub-arctic & Mediterranean. It may have grown here at the end of the last glacial period 15,000 years ago & has managed to cling on ever since. The rocky slopes must replicate in some way its favoured habitat. It's struggling to keep going though. There are about a dozen plants left & most have to be protected from cattle by electric fences.

Harebell

Yellow Bartisa at Windmill Farm

Soapy Cove & Gew-graze Valley

The valley that curves to the sea from Kynance Farm is typical of the serpentine landscape. There's hardly a plant more than knee high. It's all the more eye-catching when the valley path is sprinkled with the nodding heads of Harebells in the late summer. On the north side of the cove is the largest steatite or soapstone quarry on the Lizard. The start of the C18th saw a fashion, verging on mania, for imported Chinese porcelain. The method of manufacture was a well kept secret in China but entrepreneurs here, and in Europe, took on the search for materials that would replicate porcelain's thin, strong and semi-transparent nature. From about 1750 white crumbly talc or soapstone was quarried here and from smaller quarries at Pentreath and Mullion Cove for use in the industry. If you rub any piece of serpentine with your fingers, you will feel the soapy or greasy texture of the rock – this is why the serpentine blocks used in stiles are slippery after rain.

Rill Cove

Spanish silver coins and silver bars from an unnamed wreck of 1618 have been recovered from Rill Cove. The wreck was discovered almost by accident because it's actually overlain by another wreck, the trawler *Kerris Reed* which was lost here in 1968. Sometimes it looks as if ships were queuing up to be wrecked on the Lizard.

The cackling call of Cornish Chough can be heard all along this coast

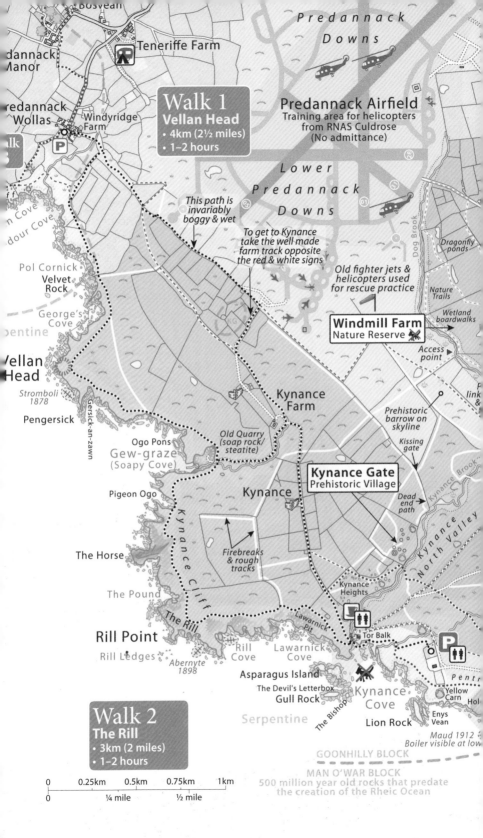

Bosvean

Predannack Downs

dannack Manor

Teneriffe Farm

redannack Wollas

Windyridge Farm

Walk 1
Vellan Head
• 4km (2½ miles)
• 1–2 hours

Predannack Airfield
Training area for helicopters
from RNAS Culdrose
(No admittance)

L o w e r
P r e d a n n a c k
D o w n s

Dog Brook

Dragonfly ponds

n Cove

dour Cove

This path is invariably boggy & wet

To get to Kynance take the well made farm track opposite the red & white signs

Old fighter jets & helicopters used for rescue practice

Nature Trails

Wetland boardwalks

Pol Cornick

Velvet Rock

George's Cove

Windmill Farm
Nature Reserve

Access point

entine

P link &

ellan Head

Stromboli 1878

Kynance Farm

Prehistoric barrow on skyline

Kissing gate

Pengersick

Gersick-an-zawn

Old Quarry (soap rock/ steatite)

Kynance Brook

Ogo Pons

Gew-graze (Soapy Cove)

Kynance Gate
Prehistoric Village

Dead end path

Pigeon Ogo

Kynance

K y n a n c e
N o r t h   V a l l e y

The Horse

Firebreaks & rough tracks

The Pound

Kynance Heights

The Rill

Kynance Cliff

Lawarnick Pit

Rill Point

Rill Ledges

Abernyte 1898

Rill Cove

Lawarnick Cove

Tor Balk

P

Pentr

Walk 2
The Rill
• 3km (2 miles)
• 1–2 hours

Asparagus Island
The Devil's Letterbox
Gull Rock

Kynance Cove

Yellow Carn

Hol

Enys Vean

Serpentine

The Bishop

Lion Rock

Maud 1912
Boiler visible at low

GOONHILLY BLOCK

MAN O'WAR BLOCK
500 million year old rocks that predate
the creation of the Rheic Ocean

0	0.25km	0.5km	0.75km	1km
0	¼ mile		½ mile	

Walk 3

West Coast of the Lizard

Predannack, Ogo-dour, Mullion Cove & Polurrian

Orchids & sea gulls

Helston
Mullion Cove
Predannack
Kynance
Lizard Point

BUS
Helston - Lizard Town bus, Mullion Cricket Club stop, 1.2km (¾ mile) from Mullion Cove.

CAR PARKING
Large public car parks at Mullion Cove & Poldhu. National Trust car park at Predannack Wollas.

FOOD & DRINKS
Pasties, food shops, cafes & pub in Mullion & cafe at Mullion Meadows. Polurrian has a beach cafe.

LOOK OUT FOR...
• Sea birds on Mullion Island and The Vro – bring some binoculars
• Take the bus to Lizard Town & take a day to walk from Lizard Point to Mullion where you can pick the bus up once more. It's about 11km (7 miles) on the coast path – a bit less if you shortcut across some of the headlands.
• Gift shops at Mullion Meadows

This is the final section before we leave the Lizard rocks behind us at **Polurrian**. At **Ogo-dour Cove** (Cornish, *ogo* is *cave*, *dour* is *water*) the cliffs change and soften. The heath-covered serpentine cliffs are replaced by the grassy slopes of schist at **Predannack Head** and they are grazed by herds of Shetland ponies. At **Predannack Morva** the path briefly drops down to a small stream and then rises dramatically back onto the serpentine of **Mullion Cliff** – the highest on the Lizard. The black serpentine cliffs make a final brief reappearance above **Porth Pyg** (Cornish, *pyk* for *beak* or *spout*) before descending towards Mullion Cove and Polurrian.

Mullion Cove
Rising sea levels and a century of storms and gales have taken their toll on the harbour and it's been decided that any major damage to the quay will not be repaired. A similar quay at Lamorna on the Land's End peninsula has already been reclaimed by the sea. Occasional boat trips leave from the harbour in the summer to view the coastline and watch the birds and seals on Mullion Island. A small tunnel runs from the harbour through the cliff to the beach at Porth Pyg.

Mullion Island

The Vro & Mullion Island
The island is a home to colonies of seabirds. Kittiwake, cormorant, razorbill, guillemot, black backed gulls and peregrine falcon all breed here. Seals haul themselves out onto the rocks to sunbathe.

Polurrian Cove

Mullion Village

This is the largest village on the peninsula and it's a thriving local community based around farming, tourism and some fishing from Mullion Cove. The large secondary school serves the whole of the Lizard peninsula. The centre has shops and galleries. It sits astride the Lizard boundary with one foot on the serpentine and one foot on the slate. It's only a short walk from the village to Mullion Cove or Polurrian and on to the coastal footpaths.

Polurrian

A huge sandy beach popular with surfers and families. Just north of **Pedn-y-ke** there's a 10 metre wide zone of shattered and crushed rock in the cliff. This is where the Lizard rocks have been faulted against the slates of Cornwall and where the Lizard block has been thrust up many kilometres from the Earth's interior.

Flora

Our friend of the festiferous sores, *Fringed Rupture-wort* that was visible below Lizard Lighthouse & on crags of schist at Pentreath makes a reappearance here along with clovers. In April the cliffs are covered in a delightful blue haze of *Spring Squill*. Also look out for *Green Winged Orchids*. Natural England and the National Trust maintain the cliff and heath habitat by grazing wild ponies and Soay sheep to keep down the grasses and increase the diversity of wild plants.

Mullion Cove

Sea Aster

Sheep's-bit

Guillemot

Razorbill

Kittiwake

Black backed gull

Cormorant

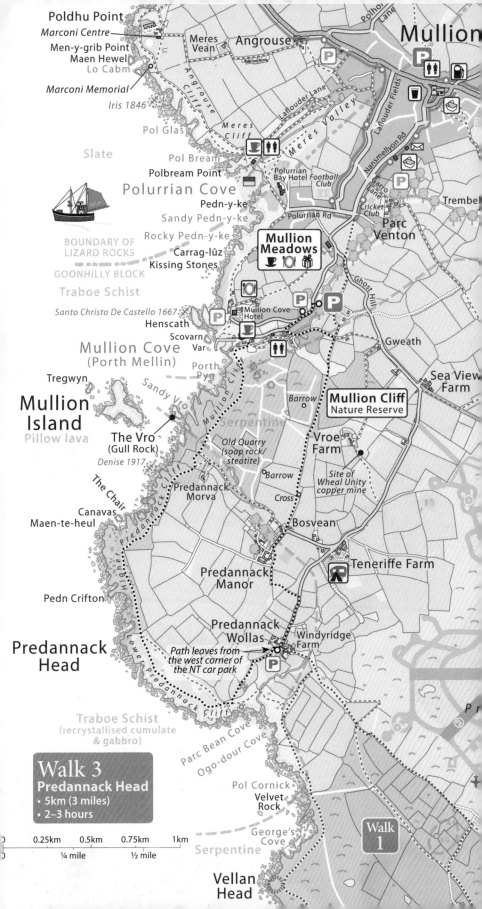

Poldhu Point
Marconi Centre
Men-y-grib Point
Maen Hewel
Lo Cabm
Marconi Memorial
Iris 1846

Meres
Vean

Angrouse

Mullion

Pol Glas
Meres Cliff
Meres Valley
Lafrouder Lane
Lafouder Fields
Slate
Pol Bream
Polbream Point
Polurrian Cove
Pedn-y-ke
Sandy Pedn-y-ke
Rocky Pedn-y-ke
Carrag-lûz
Kissing Stones

BOUNDARY OF
LIZARD ROCKS
GOONHILLY BLOCK
Traboe Schist

Santo Christo De Castello 1667
Henscath
Scovarn
Var

Mullion Cove
(Porth Mellin)

Tregwyn

**Mullion
Island**
Pillow lava

The Vro
(Gull Rock)
Denise 1917

The Chair
Canavas
Maen-te-heul

Pedn Crifton

Predannack
Head

Traboe Schist
(recrystallised cumulate
& gabbro)

Polurrian
Bay Hotel
Football
Club
Polurrian Rd

**Mullion
Meadows**

Mullion Cove
Hotel

Porth
Pyg
Serpentine
Old Quarry
(soap rock/
steatite)

Barrow

Cross

Bosvean

Predannack
Morva

Predannack
Manor

Predannack
Wollas
*Path leaves from
the west corner of
the NT car park*

Windyridge
Farm

Parc Bean Cove
Ogo-dour Cove

Pol Cornick
Velvet
Rock

George's
Cove
Serpentine

Vellan
Head

Nansmellyon Rd

Trembe

Parc
Venton

Ghost Hill

Gweath

Mullion Cliff
Nature Reserve

Sea View
Farm

Vroe
Farm

Site of
Wheal Unity
copper mine

Teneriffe Farm

Walk
1

Pr

Walk 3
Predannack Head
- 5km (3 miles)
- 2–3 hours

0.25km   0.5km   0.75km   1km
¼ mile   ½ mile

Ogo-dour Cove looking south to Vellan Head

Walk 4

Poldhu, Gunwalloe Cove, Jangye-ryn & Halzephron

The church of the storms

Helston
Loe Pool
Gunwalloe
Mullion

Lizard Point

BUS
Helston - Lizard Town bus, Mullion Golf Club or Poldhu stops & then 10min walk to Church Cove. If you're doing the walk behind Gunwalloe Marsh jump off at Cury Church – you can pick the bus up again at Poldhu.

CAR PARKING
There's a large National Trust car park behind the beach at Gunwalloe. Small car park at top of the lane from Poldhu to Carrag-a-pilez Cliff. Space for 2 or 3 cars above Halzephron Cove on the remains of the old road (the rest has disappeared over the cliff).

FOOD & DRINKS
Beach shop at Gunwalloe in the summer for take away teas. Barefoot Cafe at Halzephron House, Halzephron Inn at Chyanvounder.

LOOK OUT FOR...
- Treasure on the beach at Jangye-ryn
- Marconi Centre

The Lizard rocks give way to the glorious beaches at Polurrian, **Poldhu** and **Gunwalloe**. How very different from the brooding black cliffs of Mullion and Kynance. The cliff walk from **Poldhu** to **Gunwalloe** takes just 10 minutes but to go by car it's an 11km (7 mile) journey as the road veers inland to avoid **Gunwalloe Marsh.** We've picked a less used walk from **Cury Church Town** that passes across the top of Gunwalloe Marsh to the **Halzephron Inn** and then back along the coast to Poldhu. Although the start and finish points are both on the Poldhu to Cury road and quite close together, we haven't shown this as a circular walk because the road is narrow and busy.

Jangye-ryn & Church Cove, Gunwalloe
At least two treasure ships have been lost here. The *Schiedam* was wrecked on Jangye-ryn beach in 1684. Dozens of cannons lie on the sea bed just offshore and pewter spoons, candlesticks and coins have all been found here (Jangye-ryn is often called Dollar Cove). An unknown treasure ship spilled gold and silver coins into the cleft of a different Dollar Cove on Castle Mound and silver pieces-of-eight turn up every now and then, dislodged by storms from the rocky gullies.

Church Cove Gunwalloe

Poldhu

Poldhu & Marconi

A very popular surfing and family beach. In December 1901 the first radio signal to cross the Atlantic was sent from Poldhu to Newfoundland starting the radio revolution. The masts have long since gone, Goonhilly is the now the modern communication centre. You can still wander around the site and there's an exhibition at the Marconi Centre.

The Marconi radio station at Poldhu

Geology

The low cliffs of **Jangye-ryn** & **Porthleven** illustrate what geologists call *crustal shortening*, which not only sounds unpleasant but looks painful too. Mud laid down in horizontal layers has been squeezed into contorted folds by earth movements caused by the thrusting of the Lizard.

San Antonio
1527

Gunwalloe
Fishing Cov

Baulk Head

Park Bean (

Fabey's

Halzephr
Cove

James
Rebecca
41 drow

Above
The *Church of the Storms* at Gunwalloe Cove. The church is from the second great period of Medieval building in the C14th & C15th & is said to contain wood salvaged from the wreck of the *San Antonio* in 1527.

Below
At least two treasure ships have been wrecked at Gunwalloe. Every now & then Spanish pieces-of-eight turn up on the beach.

St Winwalloe's Church

A small, simple and beautiful Cornish church known over time as the *Church of the Storms*. It's tucked behind the small headland known as Castle Mound and has been threatened many times by the sea. St Winwalloe was born in Brittany about AD460 to the Welsh princess Gwen Teirbron or Gwen the triple-breasted because she had one breast for each of her three sons. His father was Fracan, a Celtic prince, and he grew up as a pupil of Saint Budoc of Budock Vean and Budock Water near Falmouth. He founded the monastery of Landévennec near Brest in AD485 and is revered at Landewednack near Lizard Town (possibly a straight transposition of the Breton name). There were very close links between Cornwall and Brittany at this time because of a great migration from Cornwall following a plague (or the Saxon invasions). It may be that they were even part of a single kingdom. The links were so deeply rooted that even in the early Medieval period Breton would be more understandable to a Cornishman than English.

Halzephron & the loss of the James & Rebecca

The transport ship *James & Rebecca* was returning from South America with a squadron of Light Dragoons in November 1807 when she ran into trouble below the high cliffs of Halzephron (Cornish: *als* for *cliff*, *yfarn* for *hells*). She fired her guns to attract assistance but rescuers struggled to get to her because of the height of the cliffs. During the night 100 of the 200 people on board had been hauled up the cliff to safety but by mid morning her hull gave way and all the remaining passengers and crew were thrown into the sea where 41 drowned. They're buried on the cliff top.

Walk 4
Gunwalloe Marsh
- 5.5km (3½ miles)
- 2–3 hours

Gunwalloe
Berepper
Polgrean Farm
Millewarne
Anhay Farm
...warne Mill
Chyanvounder
Burgess (abandoned)
Trenoweth Farm
Chepy (abandoned)
Halzephron House
Sowanna Farm
Transingove
Colvenno Farm
Toll
Cury White C
Hingey Farm
Chymder
Cury Churchtown
Nanfan Farm
Gwills
Gunwalloe Marsh
Busy & narrow road with no pavement
P
Winnianton
Beachshop
Clubhouse
Mullion Golf Course
Towan Cottages
...am 1684
ngye-ryn
Fishing or ...llar Cove)
Castle Mound
Dollar Cove
The Towans
37
Priske
Church Cove (Gunwalloe Beach)
Carrag-a-pilez reef
SS Grip 1887
San Salvador 1669
Jonkheer Meester Van Der Wall Putteshock 1867
Round Barrows
Polhorman Farm
Newton Farm
Poldhu Cove
P
Poldhu Point
Marconi Centre
Men-y-grib Point
Maen Hewel
Lo Cabm
Marconi Memorial
Iris 1846
Meres Vean
Angrouse
Mullion
P
P
Pol Glas
Meres Cliff
Slate
Pol Bream
Polbream Point
Polurrian Cove
Pedn-y-ke
Sandy Pedn-y-ke
Rocky Pedn-y-ke
Carrag-lûz
Kissing Stones
BOUNDARY OF LIZARD ROCKS
GOONHILLY BLOCK
Traboe Schist
Santo Christo De Castello 1667
Meres Valley
Angrouse Cliff
Lanouder Lane
Lanouder Fields
Nansmellyon Rd
Polurrian Bay Hotel
Football Club
Polurrian Rd
Cricket Club
Trembel
Parc Venton
Mullion Meadows
Ghost Hill
Mullion Cove Hotel

Scale: 0 — 0.25km — 0.5km — 0.75km — 1km
¼ mile — ½ mile

Looking over Mullion Island to Halzephron & Loe Bar from Predannack Cliff

West Coast of the Lizard

Loe Bar, Loe Pool & Helston

An estuary imprisoned

Helston

Gunwalloe

Lizard Point

BUS
Helston - Penzance bus, Penrose Hill stop or Boating Lake stop at the bottom of Helston.
If you're coming from other parts of the Lizard jump off at **Coinage Hall Street** (Blue Anchor) in Helston where you can pick up a pasty & walk down to the Boating Lake.

CAR PARKING
National Trust car parks are dotted around Loe Pool.

FOOD & DRINKS
Nothing on the walk itself but you can pick up sandwiches & pasties in Helston & Porthleven.

LOOK OUT FOR...
- Helston Folk Museum
- Yellow Horned Poppy on the bar
- The waves after a gale
- Hire a pedalo on Helston Boating Lake

BEWARE
Even on a calm day at Loe Bar large waves can take the unwary by surprise. Don't be tempted to even paddle or swim in the sea here.

The National Trust have made the area around **Loe Pool** (Cornish: *loe* is *logh* or *lake*) very open and accessible. You can walk around the whole of Loe Pool in a day but most people choose to walk smaller sections starting at one of the car parks dotted around the edge. The west side is the most popular as it follows a bumpy driveway from **Helston Boating Lake** to **Bar Lodge**. It's good enough for cycling and for pushing a buggy. A quieter, less used footpath follows the eastern side, but is only suitable for walkers.

Helston

By modern-day standards Helston is off the beaten track. Like Penzance it has many fine Georgian buildings which show the wealth that flowed through the town from the tin and copper mines. It's the nearest large town to the Lizard and has a wider range of facilities than can be found in Mullion or at Lizard Town. This includes the excellent facility of the Blue Anchor in Coinagehall Street. It brews its own beer – the famous *Spingo*, reputedly only sold in half pint measures to strangers in case it leaves them speechless and trembling with its potency. Helston's

Yellow Horned Poppy

Folk Museum is a little gem. It's housed in the old butter market and the walls are lined with old carts, a huge timber cider press and it's packed full of local archaeological finds and a great collection of 1960s cookers and radios.

Looking over Loe Bar to Loe Pool. The victims of the Anson were buried close to the memorial 'without coffin, shroud or ceremony'.

HMS Anson is wrecked

In December 1807 *HMS Anson* ran for cover into Mount's Bay and let out her anchor in the hope of riding out the storm. Her cable parted and she was picked up by the huge waves that fall on Loe Bar and dumped on the shingle, immediately breaking her back. The mast made a gangway of sorts and some of the crew made it to safety but 120 were lost, drowning close to shore in front of hundreds of onlookers who could hear their screams for help but were powerless to save them. Henry Trengrouse, who witnessed this horror, vowed to find a way to prevent disasters like the Anson recurring. His idea was to fire a rocket apparatus from the cliff or beach which would carry a line onto the stricken ship. The crew could then be brought ashore by a chair and pulley system. Known as the Rocket, it saved many hundreds of lives but has been superseded by rescue helicopters from Culdrose.

Flora of shingle

Shingle beach is a rare habitat in Cornwall. *Yellow Horned Poppy* (left) is one of the most beautiful of seaside plants. It grows on the back of the bar near the outfall. The roots of *Sea Holly* (below) were once collected & candied for sale at fairs as an aphrodisiac.

Sea Holly

Flora of shingle

Cabbages, like children, are always happy at the seaside. *Sea Kale* is a very handsome and architectural plant & always attracts the attention of children on the beach.

Down on the strand line you'll often find *Sea Rocket* – another member of the cabbage family. Its seeds are dispersed by the waves & in some years there are hundreds of plants in a single locality, but in the next year there will be none. It does well if winter storms have piled up seaweed on the strand line.

Sea Rocket

Sea Kale

SS Tripolitania 1913. The captain drove her onto Loe Bar to save the crew. She was broken up for scrap.

Loe Bar

In bad weather waves fall on Loe Bar with tremendous force – it's a great sight. The bar drops very steeply below the water so there's nothing to slow the waves down as they roll from the deep water in Mount's Bay to building and breaking on the bar. You can actually feel the vibrations through the shingle 100 metres from the sea's edge. When sailing ships were driven into Mount's Bay by a southwesterly storm they had little hope of getting out. All they could do was pay out as many anchors as possible and hope to ride out the storm before the anchors dragged or separated. Many captains, aware that they couldn't avoid being wrecked, actually chose to head for Loe Beach in preference to being driven under the high cliffs of Halzephron. At least they had a chance of rescue on Loe Bar. There are so many wrecks off Loe Bar, it's said that if the tide went right out you could walk from Porthleven Sands to Gunwalloe Fishing Cove without even touching the seabed.

Helston

St Johns

Mus

Cinema

Wendroi Trengro

St Elvan

Lanner Vean

P

Blue Anchor

Meneage Street

Boating Lake

Porthleven Road

A394

Children's Play Park

2,2A

P

Venton Vedra

Penventon

Nansloe Manor

He Ho (mino no

B3304

Higher Lanner

Lower Nansloe

Nansloe Farm

Loe Valley

Lower Lanner

Loe Marsh

Nanswidden

se Hill

Penrose House

Helston Lodge

Bird Hide

The Loe

Degibna

A3083

Little Goonhus

Higher Penrose

al Penrose Mine (Lead, disused)

Degibna Wood

Chapel

Higher Pentire

Hig Goonh

Dc

Wheal Rose Mine (Lead, disused)

Muddy path

Lower Goonhusband

P

Bar Lodge

ven Sands

Loe Pool

Lower Pentire

Tangies

Vellin-gluz Rocks

Outfall

Carminowe Creek

Little Nanspean

Anson 1781

Bar Sands

Loe Bar

Nanspean

Tripolitania 1912

P

Anson Memorial

Chyvarloe

Clies Farm

B̶r̶a̶n̶kelow 1890

Walk 5
Loe Pool & Bar
• 8.7km (5½ miles)
• 3½ hours

Berepper

| 0 | 0.25km | 0.5km | 0.75km | 1km |

| 0 | ¼ mile | ½ mile |

Berepper Cross

Gunwalloe

Porthleven Harbour

The old copper mines on the granite cliffs of Trewavas Head. In the background horizontal sheets of granite have invaded the overlying slates.

West Coast of the Lizard

Porthleven to Trewavas & Rinsey Cove

A foretaste of the granite kingdom

Lizard Point

The Land's End peninsula has been visible across Mount's Bay all the way from Lizard Point and this book ends on the granite cliffs of **Trewavas Head** and **Rinsey Cove**, with a foretaste of what's to come at Gwennap Head, Porthcurno and Land's End.

Porthleven

Porthleven seems an unpromising site for a harbour with its narrow and exposed entrance, but on this coast where shelter is absent and there are no safe anchorages, the granite breakwaters are like soft welcoming arms. One of the motivations for building the harbour was to provide safety for sailing ships driven into Mount's Bay by southwesterly gales. They had little option but to drop anchor and hope to ride out the storm, a strategy that frequently proved fatal. As a last resort some ships would even try and shelter behind Mullion Island, but a more desperate and dangerous anchorage is difficult to imagine.

As well as offering much needed shelter, the close proximity of china clay pits and tin mines enabled the harbour to prosper. Timber and coal were imported for the lead, silver and tin mines nearby and china clay, tin ore and pilchards were exported. A small fishing fleet is still active in the summer. Most of the catch is landed on the other side of Mount's Bay at Newlyn Market but fresh fish is always readily available in the shops, restaurants and pubs around the harbour. Craft shops and artists' studios have taken over the old sail lofts and warehouses. Potters and willow weavers have joined the long-established art community to make Porthleven one of the most enjoyable places to visit in West Cornwall.

BUS
Porthleven is served by the Helston - Penzance bus. Rinsey is a 1.5km (1 mile) walk from the Lion & Lamb stop at Ashton along Rinsey Lane or a 4.5km (2¾ miles) cliff walk from Porthleven.

CAR PARKING
National Trust car park above Rinsey Cove (keep to the right as you drive through Rinsey hamlet).

FOOD & DRINKS
Pubs, cafes & restaurants in Porthleven, plus the Lion & Lamb at Ashton & Queens Arms at Breage (both on A394). You can pick up sandwiches & pasties in Porthleven.

LOOK OUT FOR...
- Boat trips – look for the boards around the harbour
- Rinsey Pool – a natural swimming pool west of Trewavas Head
- The mines on Trewavas Head are as dramatic as the Crowns Mine near Botallack

29

Walk 6
Trewavas Stroll
- 2.6km (1½ miles)
- 1–2 hours

0	0.25km	0.5km	0.75km	1km

0	¼ mile	½ mile

Trewavas Head

This small dome of granite is an outlier of the main Carnmenellis boss that outcrops north of the Helford River and is visible at Merther Uny. Wherever there is granite, there are mines. The lead and silver mines of Wheal Penrose and Wheal Rose sit above Porthleven Sands. On Trewavas Head the engine houses of Trewavas Mine perch on the cliff edge. The shafts run down the cliff face to serve galleries that extend out under the seabed to the lodes of tin and copper. They are as impressive as the famous Crowns Mines at Botallack near Land's End and a provide a suitably dramatic place to end this book.

Trevallance

Stopgate   Porthleven
              Turning

St Elva

A394

2, 2A

B3304

Treza

Tranno

Tregew

Praze

Ven
Vec

Tolponds Road

Methleigh
Farm

Porthleven
School

Green Lane

Bullion Cliff

Porthleven

Parc
Trammel
Cove

Zawn Shaggy

Lower
Methleigh

Fore St

Penrose Hill

Lov
Lan

Tregear
Point

Beacon
Crag

Torleven

Sunset
Farm

Pargodonnel Rocks

Penrose
House

Zawn Cove

Giants Rock
*(Eratic rock dropped
by passing iceberg)*

Gt Trigg
Rocks

Outer Harbour

Higher
Penrose

Little Trigg
Rocks

Wheal Penrose Mine
(Lead, disused)

Harbour
Beach
St Anne 1931

Western Tye

Cviet 1884

Eastern Tye

Parc-an-als Cliff

Wheal Rose Min
(Lead, disused)

Porthleven Sands

Bar
Lodg

Vellin-gluz
Rocks

Anson 1781

Loe Bar

Tripolitania 1

Walks in this book

☐	☐	☐	

#	Walk	Distance/Time	Bus
1	Predannack, Vellan Head & Soapy Cove	4km (2½ miles) 1–2 hours	Nearest is 🚌 **Helston–Lizard bus (37)** Mullion Cricket Club stop, then 2km wal to Predannack Wollas.
2	The Rill, Gew-graze (Soapy Cove) & Kynance	3km (2 miles) 1–2 hours	🚌 **Helston–Lizard bus (37)** Lizard Green stop or jump off at Kynance Garage & walk across Lizard Downs (both add 2km) or jump off at Mullion Cricket Club & add this walk to Walk 1.
3	Predannack Head, Ogo-dour & Mullion Cove	5km (3 miles) 2–3 hours	🚌 **Helston–Lizard bus (37)** Mullion Cricket Club stop.
4	Halzephron, Gunwalloe & Cury Churchtown	5.5km (3½ miles) 2–3 hours	🚌 **Helston–Lizard bus (37)** Mullion Golf Club or Poldhu, walk to Gunwalloe, Halzephron and pick up bus again at Cury Churchtown.
5	Loe Bar & Pool	8.7km (5½ miles) 3–4 hours	🚌 **Helston–Penzance bus (2,2A)** Penrose Hill or Porthleven Rd stops.
6	Trewavas Head & Rinsey	2.6km (1½ miles) 1–2 hours	Nothing close but you could get the 🚌 **Helston–Penzance bus (2,2A)** & get off at the Lion & Lamb at Ashton. Then 2km (1¼ mile) walk to Rinsey hamlet, & walk back to Porthleven on coast path.

The Village Restaurant

01326 241007

6.3pm →